BACKYARD ANIMALS

Picture credits

R.E. Barber — Endpages; Pages 6, 19, 20-21, 27
Bill Beatty — Pages 10, 29
Rick & Nora Bowers — Page 11
Cathy & Gordon Illg — Pages 7, 18, 20
Breck P. Kent — Pages 14, 17
Dwight R. Kuhn — Pages 6, 7, 12, 13, 16, 21, 26, 28-29
Tom & Pat Leeson — Pages 10, 18, 22, 22-23, 24, 25, 26, 26-27, 29
Zig Leszczynski — Pages 14, 20, 22
Robert & Linda Mitchell — Pages 12, 13, 24-25, 25
A.B. Sheldon — Pages 15, 17
Lynn M. Stone — Page 12
Gary Vestal — Page 16
John Cancalosi/DRK — Pages 11, 21
Marty Cordano/DRK — Pages 6, 13
R.J. Erwin/DRK — Pages 8-9
Jeff Foott/DRK — Page 8
Bob Gurr/DRK — Page 27
Stephen J. Krasemann/DRK — Pages 9, 29
Dwight R. Kuhn/DRK — Pages 9, 23
Wayne Lankinen/DRK — Page 11
Andy Rouse/DRK — Page 28
George J. Sanker/DRK — Page 24
Lynn M. Stone/DRK — Page 11
Bob Firth/International Stock — Cover
Bob Jacobson/International Stock — Page 26
Earl Kogler/International Stock — Page 28
Buddy Mays/International Stock — Page 7
S. Myers/International Stock — Page 20
Joel Arrington/Visuals Unlimited — Pages 24-25
Callahan/Visuals Unlimited — Page 8
Jeffrey Howe/Visuals Unlimited — Pages 12, 15
Ken Lucas/Visuals Unlimited — Page 17
S. Maslowski/Visuals Unlimited — Page 22
J.L. McAlonan/Visuals Unlimited — Page 11
Joe McDonald/Visuals Unlimited — Page 24
Glenn M. Oliver/Visuals Unlimited — Page 19
Rob Simpson/Visuals Unlimited — Page 23
Richard Walters/Visuals Unlimited — Page 8
W.J. Weber/Visuals Unlimited — Page 9
Ken Deitcher/The Wildlife Collection — Page 17
Henry Holdsworth/The Wildlife Collection — Pages 18-19
Tim Laman/The Wildlife Collection — Page 15

Copyright © 1998
Kidsbooks, Inc.
3535 West Peterson Ave.
Chicago, IL 60659

Manufactured in the United States of America

EYES ON NATURE

BACKYARD ANIMALS

Written by
Kerry Acker

kidsbooks Incorporated

WATCHING WILDLIFE

There's a zoo on the loose just outside your door! Backyard animals play, eat, sleep, preen, prowl after one another, and raise their babies. To see all this happen, you need only to open your eyes to nature.

LOOKING AT YOU

Have you ever heard a grasshopper making music, or seen a bird pause on a branch with a bug in its beak? Animals can see, hear, and smell *you*, too. If you want to observe them, you must be nearly invisible, or they may run away. Wear clothes that aren't too bright, hide behind trees, stay downwind, and, most of all, be quiet.

DO NOT DISTURB

Imagine someone tearing down the walls of your room and carrying your possessions across town. Animals have living quarters, too. When you watch these creatures, try to be respectful of their space. Don't stand close to nesting birds, touch spider webs, or carry off rocks that serve as shelter.

6

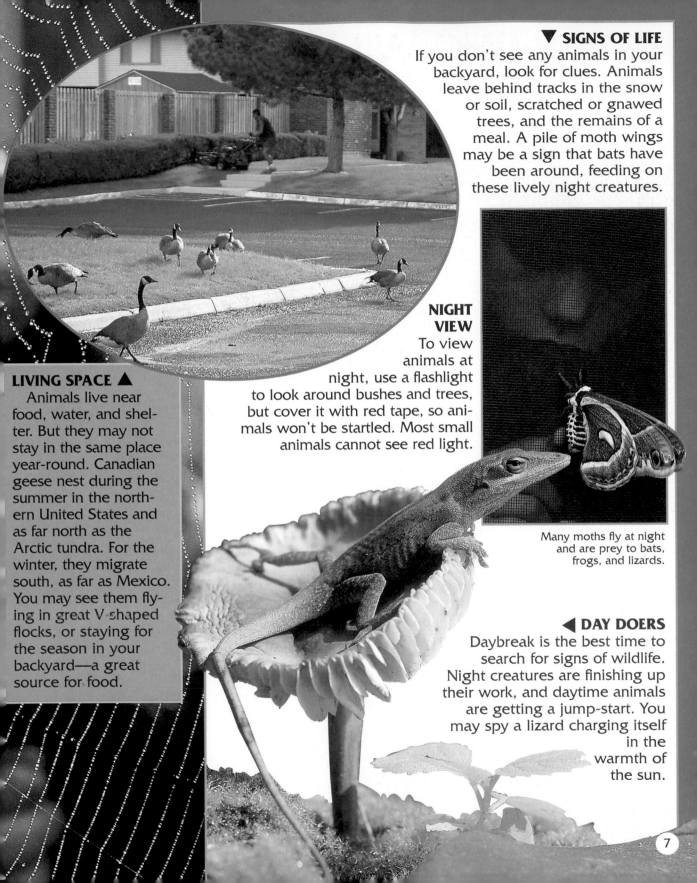

▼ SIGNS OF LIFE

If you don't see any animals in your backyard, look for clues. Animals leave behind tracks in the snow or soil, scratched or gnawed trees, and the remains of a meal. A pile of moth wings may be a sign that bats have been around, feeding on these lively night creatures.

NIGHT VIEW

To view animals at night, use a flashlight to look around bushes and trees, but cover it with red tape, so animals won't be startled. Most small animals cannot see red light.

LIVING SPACE ▲

Animals live near food, water, and shelter. But they may not stay in the same place year-round. Canadian geese nest during the summer in the northern United States and as far north as the Arctic tundra. For the winter, they migrate south, as far as Mexico. You may see them flying in great V-shaped flocks, or staying for the season in your backyard—a great source for food.

Many moths fly at night and are prey to bats, frogs, and lizards.

◄ DAY DOERS

Daybreak is the best time to search for signs of wildlife. Night creatures are finishing up their work, and daytime animals are getting a jump-start. You may spy a lizard charging itself in the warmth of the sun.

7

BUZZING BACKYARD

Even the smallest patch of yard comes alive with the buzzing and chirping of insects as they fly about, crawl creepily, and simply hang out. These little critters are both pests and helpers to humans. What would a backyard be without them?

▲ CICADA CHORUS

The cicada has an amazing life cycle. Periodical cicadas live underground for 17 years as nymphs (the stage after hatching from eggs). When the whole population crawls above ground and becomes adults, they live for only a month, "singing," mating, and laying eggs. This buzzing chorus can be heard a mile away!

▲ PEST PATROL

Ladybird beetles, also known as ladybugs, provide pest relief to farmers and gardeners by preying on mealybugs, mites, and other plant-killing insects.

◄ OUT FOR BLOOD

Most people agree that mosquitoes are pests. But these bugs don't bite just to bother us. Although female mosquitoes eat nectar, they need blood to help their eggs develop. After drinking your blood, a female lays her eggs—up to 500 of them!

▲ FIDDLING FELLOWS

You may not have ever seen a katydid—the green, long-legged relative of the cricket—but, chances are, you've heard one on a hot summer night. To attract females, males rub a sharp file on one wing against a scraper on the other wing, like a violinist moving a bow over a string. The raspy sound is music to female katydids.

8

▲ BEE GOOD

Bees keep your backyard beautiful. Attracted to bright colors, bees land on flowers to feed on nectar. While they suck the sweet syrup, they pick up pollen grains and store them in baskets on their hind legs. Then they carry the grains to other flowers and pollinate them, causing the flowers to produce more seeds.

FIERY FELLOW ▶

Most ants are harmless, often crawling unnoticed between your toes as you sit in the backyard. But the red fire ant bites and injects venom, causing a burning sensation. This native of Brazil came to the United States in the 1930s, aboard ships. When they arrived, they multiplied and kept traveling.

9

▲ TWO-EYED TWIG

During the day, if you look closely in trees or shrubs, you just might spot a two-eyed twig! Stick insects avoid predators by sitting motionless. Usually long and thin, they are tree-green, leaf-brown, or any color that helps them blend into their background.

WINGED WONDERS

Your backyard is bursting with signs of bird life—baby-blue robins' eggs, nests of soft lichens and spider threads, birds big and small rustling about in treetops. Listen closely to their calls. You'll be surprised at how many different birds live in your own backyard!

EARLY BIRD ▼

Have you ever been the first to wake up? Probably not before the robin. As the sun rises, so does the robin, greeting the new day with its morning music, which sounds something like "cheer-up, cheer-up."

KNOCK, ▶ KNOCK!

That knocking you hear in the woods is probably a woodpecker. This tiny, downy bird climbs up trees using its stiff tail feathers and two pincerlike feet. With the help of its chisel-like bill, the bird chips away wood, then sticks out a long, slimy, barb-filled tongue, spearing its insect lunch.

HAWK HUNTERS ▶

The Cooper's hawk waits patiently to snare squirrels and other small animals. When food becomes scarce in the fall, these birds of prey fly south, often joining up with other species of hawks. Their mass migration over the Appalachian Mountains is one of the most spectacular sights to bird enthusiasts.

AQUA-BATICS

Go to a lake, and you may spot a grebe (GREEB). Grebes are great swimmers, gliding gracefully among reeds. When frightened, they sink quietly underwater, leaving just their neck and head above the surface.

TRAWLING FOR TRASH

Herring gulls, or seagulls, don't just chase ferries and hang out by the seashore. These scavengers feed at garbage dumps and in crowded cities. They also eat freshly caught mollusks, dropping them from high in the sky onto hard surfaces to crack open the shells.

▲ SWEET TREATS

As the hummingbird hovers above a brightly colored flower, it sips nectar at 13 licks per second. Its wings beat as fast as 78 times per second. These are the only birds that can fly backwards!

COOING COURTSHIP

The mourning dove gets its name from the male's sad "cooo, cooo." Actually, this call is an important part of courting. During courtship, the male soars high in the sky and then swoops down, making big, sweeping circles before returning to his perch beside the female.

11

CREEPY CRAWLERS

Many of the smallest, creepy crawlers have an important job to do in your backyard. But some crawlers also do harm to plants and need to be controlled. Look closely, and see how many slithering, creepy crawlers you can find!

▲ This prickly caterpillar will eventually change into a saddleback moth.

▼ TOIL IN THE SOIL

Earthworms play an essential role in keeping your backyard bountiful and beautiful. Acting as little underground farmers, they turn over soil, putting air and nutrients into it. This enables plants to grow.

▲ ACH! AN ARACHNID!

Daddy longlegs, also called harvestmen, have eight very long, skinny legs. They belong to the same class as spiders—arachnids. Harvestmen eat plant juices, insects, and even other daddy longlegs.

BUSY MUNCHERS

Caterpillars are larvae hatched from butterfly eggs. These creepy creatures crawl all over plants, munching away at leaves, because they need a lot of food to make the big change into butterflies.

▼ SLIME TIME

Slugs can damage gardens, chewing holes in fruit, flowers, and leaves. These slimy creatures move along by stretching their body, sometimes to eleven times their normal length! They secrete a path of mucus, cleverly marking their own scent so they can find their way home when it's dark out.

▼ The banana slug

▼ LOTS O' LEGS

These leggy crawlers love to lurk in damp places around your house, feeding at night on insects. The female centipede covers her eggs with a sticky juice and rolls them around in dirt. This prevents the male from eating them!

▶ SNAIL TRAIL

Snails move around in a really weird way. Active mostly at night in moist areas such as gardens, snails secrete a slimy substance and move over it by contracting their muscular "foot." If you see silver streaks on plant leaves in the early morning, that's a snail trail!

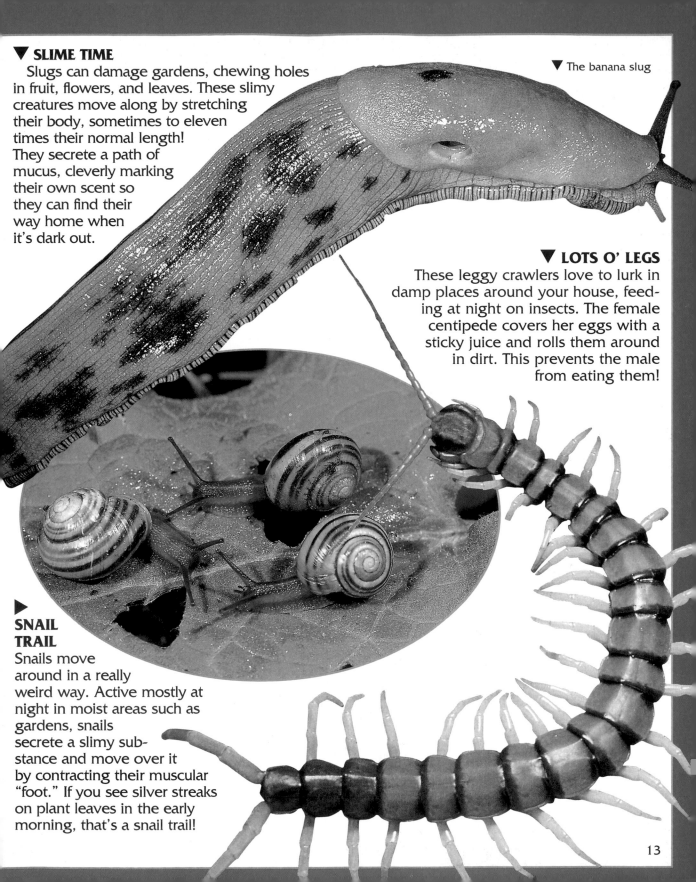

COOL CHARACTERS

Reptiles and amphibians may not be cuddly creatures, and some are even dangerous to touch, but many are gentle and safe to observe up close.

SILENT SALAMANDER

When on a backyard adventure, lift up rocks or leaves. You might surprise an unsuspecting salamander hidden underneath! These smooth-skinned amphibians sneak about quietly in woods and shallow water. The one shown here is guarding her eggs.

LITTLE BULL ▶

"Jug o' rum, more rum," croaks Earth's largest frog, the bullfrog. Bullfrogs hang out at night by ponds or lakes. Look for their big, bulging eyes. If you catch a bullfrog, it might try to trick you and play dead, hanging motionless and limp.

LEAPIN' ◀ LIZARDS

Collared lizards, dwelling in rocky, sandy areas of the Southwest, are some of the fastest reptiles, speeding up to 17 miles an hour. As with other lizards, when grabbed from behind, their tail breaks off and keeps wiggling, fooling the pursuer while the lizard flees. Luckily, another tail grows in its place!

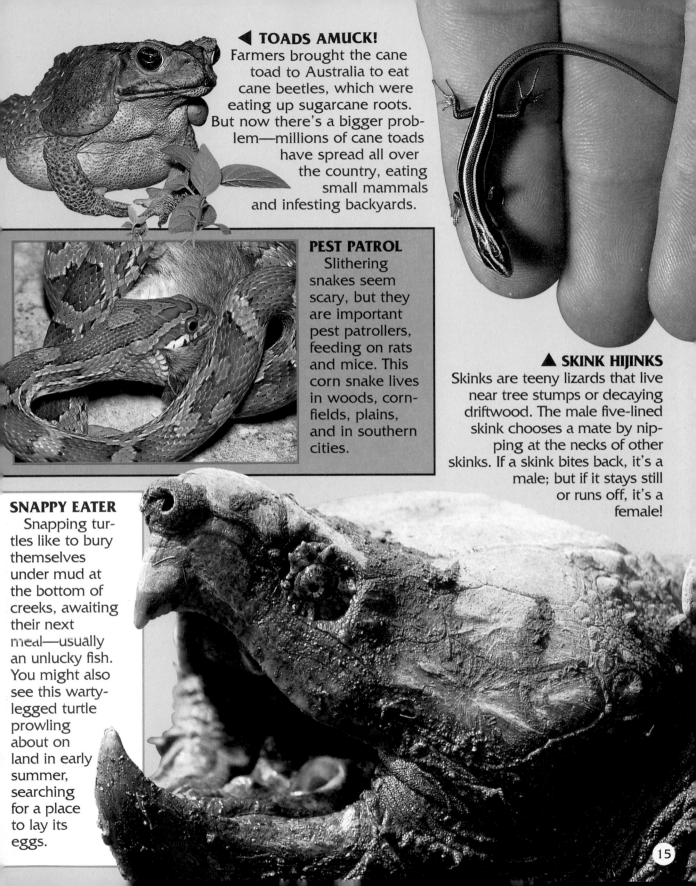

◀ TOADS AMUCK!

Farmers brought the cane toad to Australia to eat cane beetles, which were eating up sugarcane roots. But now there's a bigger problem—millions of cane toads have spread all over the country, eating small mammals and infesting backyards.

PEST PATROL

Slithering snakes seem scary, but they are important pest patrollers, feeding on rats and mice. This corn snake lives in woods, cornfields, plains, and in southern cities.

▲ SKINK HIJINKS

Skinks are teeny lizards that live near tree stumps or decaying driftwood. The male five-lined skink chooses a mate by nipping at the necks of other skinks. If a skink bites back, it's a male; but if it stays still or runs off, it's a female!

SNAPPY EATER

Snapping turtles like to bury themselves under mud at the bottom of creeks, awaiting their next meal—usually an unlucky fish. You might also see this warty-legged turtle prowling about on land in early summer, searching for a place to lay its eggs.

BEAUTY IN FLIGHT

Some of the most colorful, delicate animals in the back-yard, butterflies float from flower to flower in search of their next meal of nectar or pollen. Moths, their relatives, may not be as brightly colored, but that's because they mostly come out at night.

This swallowtail butterfly feeds on a sunflower.

A camouflaged green, the luna moth is amazing to see.

◀ WEIRD UP CLOSE

They may look pretty from a dis-tance, but butterflies and moths look strange up close. They have a head, antennae, six legs, a body in two parts, scales, and thousands of eyes, called com-pound eyes, that allow them to see all around them at once.

16

THE FIRST CHANGES ▶

The metamorphosis (meh-tuh-MORE-fuh-sus) of a caterpillar into a butterfly seems magical. Hatched from an egg, the caterpillar sheds its skin as it grows. Then it attaches itself to a twig with silk, and its skin forms a hardened shell called a *chrysalis*. Some moth caterpillars wrap themselves inside a silk case called a *cocoon*. After weeks, or even months, a butterfly or moth breaks out, dries itself, and takes off in search of food and a mate.

The cecropia moth

MONARCH MIGRATION

Butterflies and moths have a short life—some live for only a few days, others as long as 10 months! Some that live through a change of seasons will migrate. In the fall, monarchs travel nearly 2,000 miles from the north to warmer climates in California, Florida, and Texas. Quite a spectacle, these large groups gather in trees to hibernate for the winter.

MAGIC DUST?

If a butterfly lights on your hand, be careful not to touch its wings. If you do, you'll find that a very fine dust rubs off on your skin. Although not dangerous to you, the loss of this dust could be bad for the butterfly, because it consists of the very small scales that cover the insect's body. Scales may be very plain or very colorful, or may form intricate designs on the wings.

The regal moth

BACKYARD SURPRISE

There's nothing quite like seeing beautiful or bizarre animals appear suddenly in your backyard. Try your very best to be gentle and quiet. If frightened, a visitor such as the white-tailed deer will raise its tail and flee.

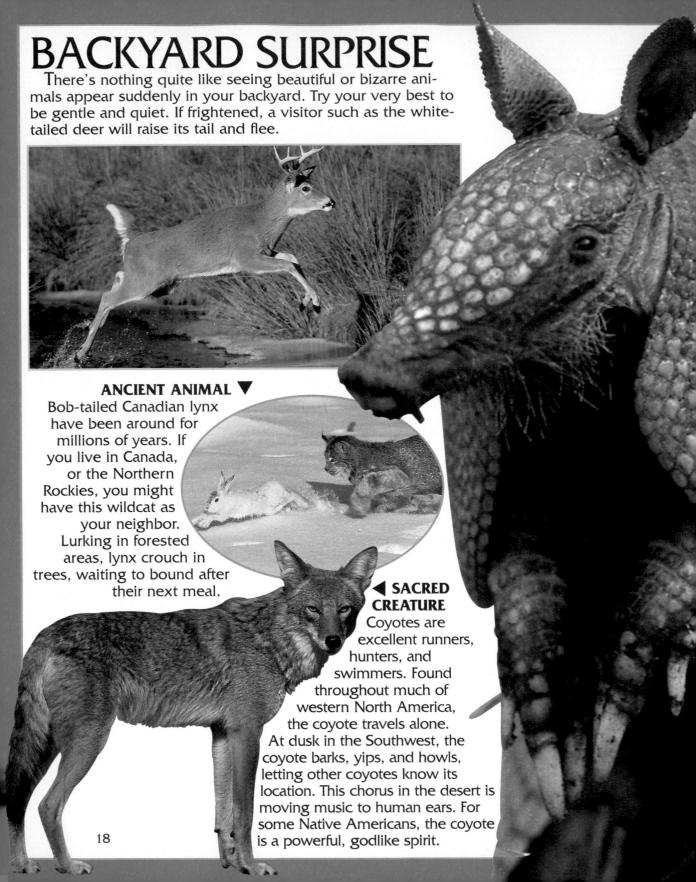

ANCIENT ANIMAL ▼

Bob-tailed Canadian lynx have been around for millions of years. If you live in Canada, or the Northern Rockies, you might have this wildcat as your neighbor. Lurking in forested areas, lynx crouch in trees, waiting to bound after their next meal.

◄ SACRED CREATURE

Coyotes are excellent runners, hunters, and swimmers. Found throughout much of western North America, the coyote travels alone. At dusk in the Southwest, the coyote barks, yips, and howls, letting other coyotes know its location. This chorus in the desert is moving music to human ears. For some Native Americans, the coyote is a powerful, godlike spirit.

▼ HARD BODY

Is that an armored tank? Wrong! It's an armadillo, a small mammal covered with hard, bony plates, with skin in between that lets the creature twist and curl. The nine-banded armadillo lives in the southeastern United States, rooting for insects or vegetables, and eating with its pointy, sticky tongue.

DESERT DWELLERS

Kids with homes by the southwest desert might count the javelina as a backyard buddy. A piglike creature with sharp tusks, the javelina exudes a skunky odor, making it easier for other javelinas to find it.

MASSIVE MOOSE

The moose, the world's largest deer, has a stomach that can hold 112 pounds of food. Found in the northern United States, Canada, Europe, and Asia, moose often gather together during winter, feeding on bushes and willows, and sometimes wander into a backyard. Male moose are recognizable by their enormous antlers, which they shed in December.

FURRY FORAGERS

Even the critters you find cutest can do damage to your lawn, flower patch, or garden. Others might raid your garbage.

DIG THIS ▲

Badgers build elaborate habitats. Using sharp claws, they dig burrow systems, or setts, in forests or other sheltered areas. Badgers keep their homes really clean. Each sett has a separate area for sleeping, breeding, and even "going to the bathroom." Sometimes, badgers use the same home that their grandparents lived in!

HOP ALONG ▲

Cuddly cottontail rabbits may look cute, hopping around your yard. But they do something that you might think is disgusting—they eat their own droppings! Actually, the bunny is being healthy, because its body gets more nutrients when its food is digested twice.

BOXING BUNNIES

Hares are oversized rabbits, equipped with long ears, very thick fur, and strong hind legs that help them run up to 35 miles an hour and jump 6 1/2 feet high! Male brown hares have an interesting way of winning a female's affection. They play-fight another male, chasing, kicking, and "boxing," until one of them gives up.

WILY WEASELS ▼

Like many other mammals, weasels are carnivores. Sneaky hunters, weasels occasionally rob eggs, but a tasty mouse meal is always lip-smacking good to them. So a weasel near your house means one less mouse!

THE NOSE KNOWS

One of the funniest-looking creatures in the world lives only in North America, and maybe in your backyard! The star-nosed mole sports a "star nose," or ring of 22 pink, fleshy feelers. This ground habitant scrounges for food in ponds and on soil, its star nose moving about, feeling for insect larvae and earthworms.

EGG-CEPTIONAL

Echidnas, dwelling near Australian backyards, are spiny, ant-sucking creatures that have spellbound scientists for years. Although they are warm-blooded like mammals, they lay leathery eggs—like those of reptiles. Scientists created a whole new mammal category just for the echidna and its relative, the platypus.

▲ REAL STINKERS

When a skunk is startled, it stamps its feet, turns its back, and raises its tail—and out squirts a horrible, stinking liquid! Skunks can fire six rounds of this putrid juice. So if you spot a skunk toddling around, remain still, because the skunk may interpret your quick movements as threatening behavior.

GNAW-IT-ALLS

Rodents have large, sharp teeth—perfect for gnawing and cutting. These teeth are constantly growing. Rodents have to gnaw every day to keep them short. If you see chewed-up tree trunks, you know who the culprits are! But rodents also eat insects and weeds, improving the look of your yard and freeing it from pests.

CHUBBY CHEEKS ▼

Chipmunks chatter, chirp, and whistle, but their high-pitched "chip-chip" gave them their name. Chipmunks spend their days stuffing their cheek pouches with seeds, nuts, and fruit. A chipmunk can hold up to four nuts in each chubby cheek pouch!

BRILLIANT BUILDERS

At night, busy beavers gnaw on young trees, then haul, roll, or drag them downriver, their paddlelike tails helping them swim. Using stones, mud, and branches, these clever craftsmen construct dams, creating ponds where they build their dome-shaped lodge.

FATTENING UP ▼

Woodchucks, also known as groundhogs and whistle pigs, hibernate, or sleep, during winter. In summer months, they eat plenty of food, gorging themselves on plants and sometimes vegetables from your garden.

TALL TAILS

The gray squirrel has a big, bushy tail that helps it move, maintain balance, stay warm, and even communicate. When a squirrel senses an enemy, it flashes its tail to warn other squirrels. When a squirrel falls from a tree, the tail acts like a parachute. In the rain, the tail is an umbrella!

HOUSE MOUSE

Like its rat cousins, the house mouse will chew, suck, and eat almost anything, carefully clenching its meal in its front paw and gnawing with sharp front teeth. Mice love grains, but they'll also eat strings, paper, and even cable wire!

STICKY SITUATION ▲

The porcupine may be clumsy and slow, but it has an amazing way of protecting itself. When surprised, the porcupine will bristle up its 30,000 sharp spines, or long hairs, and slash its tail, sticking the enemy with the dangerous points. Porcupines love salt, and often gnaw on tools that have been held by sweaty palms.

23

NIGHT CREATURES

Many animals spend daylight hours resting. When night falls, an entire world springs into action, filling your backyard with hisses and howls. All of these night creatures have special abilities for locating food and finding their way around in the dark.

CUTE BANDITS

Raccoons live all over the United States and in parts of Canada and South America, lumbering about at night, or squealing loudly while furiously fighting each other. These masked rascals have very flexible hands and fingers—they can remove lids, turn doorknobs, and even open refrigerators!

FLY-BY-NIGHT ▲

That animal gliding from tree to tree at night may not be a bat. The flying squirrel's legs are connected to one another with a layer of furry skin. It jumps, stretches out its legs like a sail or a parachute, brakes with its tail, and lands safely and gently on all fours.

WHITE-WASH

It may be difficult to spot owls. Their coloring blends in with the background of their nest, helping them to hide from enemies. The snowy owl has wonderful white feathers, with some dark strips.

POINTS OF LIGHT

See those yellow-green lights that flicker on warm summer nights? Fireflies, or lightning bugs, use their glowing light to send secret mating messages to other fireflies. When a female lightning bug sees a male flashing his signals, she waits a few seconds, then shines her own light back.

EARS THAT SEE

That squeak you hear may be a bat! A bat sends out high squeaks that bounce off objects—such as moths. The bat then hears the echo, and is able to detect what the object is and where it's located. Flying at night, bats need this special sense, called *echolocation*.

STUCK LIKE GLUE

Tree frogs spend their life in trees. Long, slender legs help them balance on branches, and suctionlike pads "glue" them to leaves. These pads are great for sticking to rough or smooth surfaces, so tree frogs can easily sit on top of leaves, or even cling to the bottom.

PLAYING DEAD

Opossums are gentle animals. When surprised by a predator, the opossum rolls over on its side, with its mouth wide open and eyes looking lifeless, pretending to be dead—sometimes for hours! When the attacker loses interest and leaves, the opossum "recovers" and runs away.

THAT'S WILD!

The wildest of wildlife, some animals appear in the backyard only rarely. Rattlesnakes once slithered all over the United States. Now, after years of being hunted for their skin and venom, these poisonous snakes are rare sights.

SEE YOU LATER!▼

Although they move awkwardly on land, American alligators cause quite a stir when they show up in backyards and on golf courses! Usually these creatures stay put—in saltwater swamps and brackish water in the southeastern United States.

WOLF PACKS

Gray wolves used to roam all over North America, traveling in packs. When prey was scarce in the wild, they often wandered into human settlements and attacked livestock. People killed many of them, and the wolf population shrank dramatically. Now, wildlife biologists are bringing the wolf population back, reintroducing them to natural environments, such as Yellowstone National Park.

CHICKEN-CHASER

The bobcat, which gets its name from its short, stubby tail, roams in swamps, deserts, mountains, and forested areas throughout North America. But it's hardly ever seen. Its fur provides camouflage, and it does most of its work at night, ambushing hares or birds, and maybe even chickens.

26

BEAR FACTS

Those black bears hanging around out back aren't lost. They've come with a purpose—to eat your food! American black bears don't mind living by humans. It's convenient, because there are always garbage cans to tip over, or maybe even a tasty morsel to steal from the grill.

▼ RED ROVER

Despite our hunting and trapping them, red foxes have survived. These members of the dog family are cunning, clever, and cautious. By day, they usually hide in their burrow or a hollow tree. At night, they come out to hunt gophers, rabbits, and other small animals.

BIG CAT

Only slightly smaller than a jaguar, the cougar is the second-largest cat in the Americas, growing to 160 pounds. With long canine teeth, retractable claws, and powerful limbs, this cat is a skillful and deadly predator of deer.

ANIMAL ATTRACTIONS

If you really want to see nature, learn how to attract animals to your backyard. Fountains, feeders, houses, and seeds can lure furry and feathered friends into view.

TASTY TREATS

There are certain foods that can entice certain creatures. Rabbits crave carrots, cabbage, and lettuce, while squirrels nibble on all sorts of nuts. Badgers just love to suck sticky, sweet honey. Leave some of these treats out in the yard, and see who'll come by for a snack.

◀ WATER WORKS

Animals need water to survive. A fountain or a birdbath is a great way to bring thirsty birds closer to you. You may get deer, foxes, or even wilder visitors!

BIRDHOUSE ROCK

Houses and feeders bring robins and other birds to your yard. To attract hummingbirds, put some water mixed with a little sugar into a bright red feeder. Hang the feeder where you can watch easily, but be careful not to put it too close to a window. A bird might fly at its own image and be injured.

28

DAMAGE CONTROL

It's great to have animals around, but some of them can do a lot of damage to a garden or lawn. Rabbit, deer, and other munchers will chew on cabbage, green beans, flowers, and lawn grass. People often resort to putting up fences around their yard.

A HELPING HAND

When baby animals or injured wildlife show up in your backyard, your first instinct may be to run out and pick them up. Wait! Mother animals may be nearby, looking for their lost baby. Injured animals may bite or scratch you. Consult a parent first, and call the local veterinarian. Then, if you can, lend a helping hand.

PUT A LID ON IT

Raccoons and foxes are garbage lovers. To avoid their making a mess, use sturdy metal garbage cans with tight lids, and secure the cans with cords. Hanging rags soaked in ammonia close to the cans will also help to keep these rascals away.

29